Wayfarers Walk

Hampshire
Recreation

Wayfarers Walk

Linda Herbst

John Cann

Roger Lambert

Langstone mill

Hampshire County Recreation
North Hill Close, Andover Road, Winchester, Hampshire SO22 6AQ

Distribution
Countryside Books
3 Catherine Road, Newbury, Berkshire RG14 7NA

First published October 1988

ISBN 0 948176 04 0

Design
Compass Publications
'Gull Cottage', 36 Preston Parade, Seasalter,
Whitstable, Kent CT5 4AD

Typesetting
P & J Curtis
The Gables, Highstead, Chislet, Canterbury, Kent CT3 4LX

Printed in Great Britain
A & R Colour Printers
The Oast Publicity Centre, Perry Court, London Road,
Faversham, Kent ME13 8RY

Contents

HAMPSHIRE

Inkpen
Beacon

East End
Kingsclere
Hannington
North
Oakley
Basingstoke
Overton
Deane
Whitchurch
Dummer

Andover

Micheldever
Brown
Candover
Alton
Totford
Abbotstone
New
Alresford
Tichborne
Cheriton
Hinton
Ampner
Kilmeston

Winchester

Petersfield

Romsey

Eastleigh
Droxford
Soberton
Hambledon
WEST
SUSSEX
Southampton
Denmead

Bedhampton
Fareham
Havant
Emsworth
Langstone
Gosport
Portsmouth
Hayling
Island

The Solent

Farnborough
Fleet
Aldershot

ISLE OF WIGHT

by a mile long ditch and rampart. The earthworks make use of the steep slope of the hill to provide additional defence. Wander over the camp if you have time, to get a better idea of its situation on this exposed, windy, spacious hilltop. On a clear day St. Catherine's Hill near Winchester is visible.

Combe Gibbet marks one end of the Wayfarer's Walk on the top of Berkshire's Inkpen Beacon. The gibbet — a modern replica — stands on a very large neolithic barrow above Gallows Down. The first gibbet was probably erected in the late 17th century but has been replaced several times since then. According to local legend a Combe man and his mistress were hanged here after plotting — successfully — the death of his wife. The authorities in Winchester refused to come such a distance so the villagers went to Newbury where the case was dealt with. Berkshire then asked for and received the parish of Combe to pay for all their trouble.

When Combe was in Hampshire the County boundary was the Ridgeway, and some people still consider it such even though the change was made in an 1882 local government act. The present boundary (see the O.S. map) does seem odd. The late Brian Vesey-Fitzgerald — antiquarian, historian and naturalist — writing in 1949 about Inkpen Beacon said that "Spiritually, geologically, in every way but cartographically it is still in Hampshire: geographically, too (despite what the maps say), for Inkpen is the natural frontier on the north". So perhaps the Wayfarer's Walk really begins or ends in Hampshire after all.

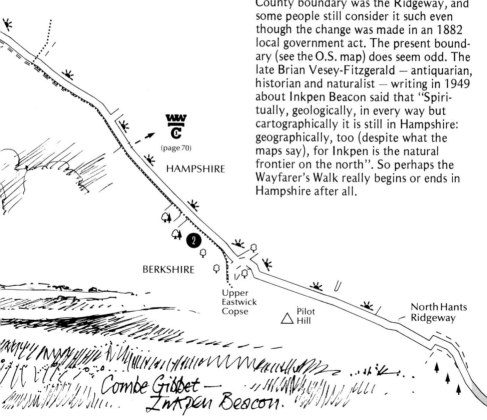

(page 70)

HAMPSHIRE

BERKSHIRE

Upper
Eastwick
Copse

Pilot
Hill

North Hants
Ridgeway

Combe Gibbet —
Inkpen Beacon.

Highclere Castle

Highclere Castle, with its pilasters, towers and turrets (not visible until nearing the A343), is the largest mansion in Hampshire. Sir Nikolaus Pevsner describes as a "perfect park" the grounds laid out by Capability Brown for the owner, Henry Herbert, in the 1770's. Henry Herbert was made Earl of Carnarvon in 1793. In the 1840's Sir Charles Barry, who designed the Palace of Westminster, converted the 18th century house into a castle for the third Earl by covering it with a Victorian gothic exterior and adding a central tower. In the grounds — besides a 'temple', summer house and chapel — are very old oaks, beeches, cedars of Lebanon, and Highclere's famed rhododendrons.

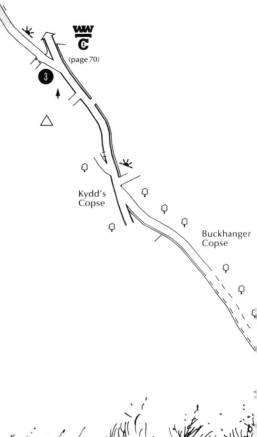

(page 70)

Kydd's Copse

Buckhanger Copse

Grotto Lodge - Highclere Estate.

North Hants Ridgeway

The North Hants Ridgeway is called the Inkpen Ridgeway as it passes through Berkshire and Wiltshire. The views from this trackway are superb, though obstructed in places by a hedge that may be as much as 500 years old.

A method of calculating the age of an old hedge is to count the number of shrub species in a 30 metre stretch. One hundred years can be reckoned for every species, though local customs and conditions can influence the result. Three 'tests' along the Wayfarer's Walk here consistently revealed ash, hawthorn, oak, blackthorn, hazel and elder, and occasionally crab apple and wild rose. The hedge coincides with an old parish boundary (between the A343 and the lane at Wychpits) — a further suggestion of its age.

We have the pheasant to thank for the survival of this green and leafy landscape as shooting them is a regular pastime in Highclere. Seven thousand birds are reared every year in ideal conditions — rich, broad-leaved woodland, some parkland, fields, thick hedgerows and two lakes. North Hampshire is an area of large estates and unfortunately some new landowners — increasingly financial institutions — want to sell woodland to grow more profitable crops. Permission is required to cut down more than 825 cu.ft. of timber (about 10 big oaks) a quarter. From 1979-80 Basingstoke District Council was notified of proposals by financial insti-tutions owning land in the district to fell 7,000 trees.

The sixth Earl lived at Highclere Castle until his death in 1987. His father, the fifth Earl (1866-1923) achieved world-wide fame when he and Howard Carter discovered the Tomb of Tutankhamun in Egypt. He had a passion for racehorses and started the renowned Highclere Stud in 1902. He was, according to his son, "one of the best shots in Europe". The seventh Earl is also a keen race-goer and has been Racing Manager to the Queen since 1969.

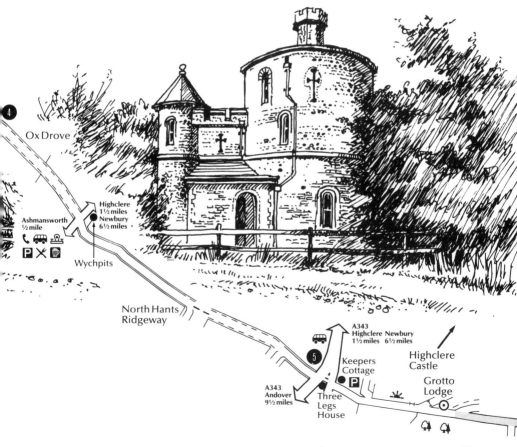

4

Ox Drove

Ashmansworth ½ mile

Highclere 1½ miles
Newbury 6½ miles

Wychpits

North Hants Ridgeway

A343 Andover 9½ miles

5

A343 Highclere Newbury 1½ miles 6½ miles

Keepers Cottage

Three Legs House

Highclere Castle

Grotto Lodge

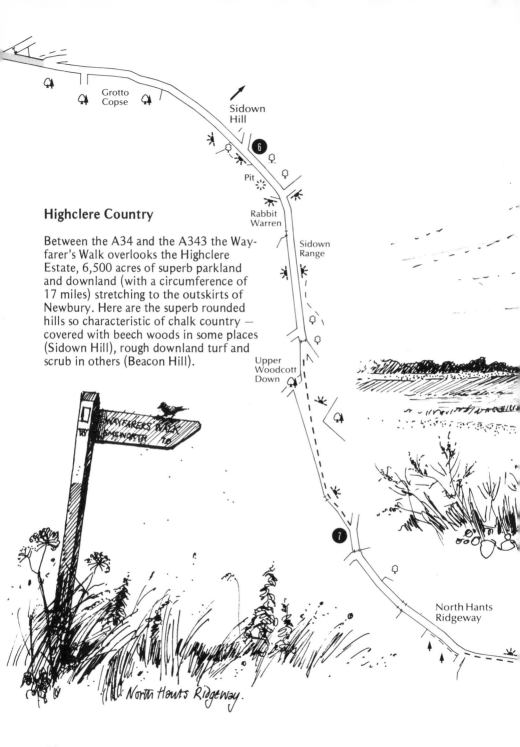

Grotto
Copse

Sidown
Hill

6

Pit

Highclere Country

Between the A34 and the A343 the Wayfarer's Walk overlooks the Highclere
Estate, 6,500 acres of superb parkland
and downland (with a circumference of
17 miles) stretching to the outskirts of
Newbury. Here are the superb rounded
hills so characteristic of chalk country —
covered with beech woods in some places
(Sidown Hill), rough downland turf and
scrub in others (Beacon Hill).

Rabbit
Warren

Sidown
Range

Upper
Woodcott
Down

7

North Hants
Ridgeway

North Hants Ridgeway.

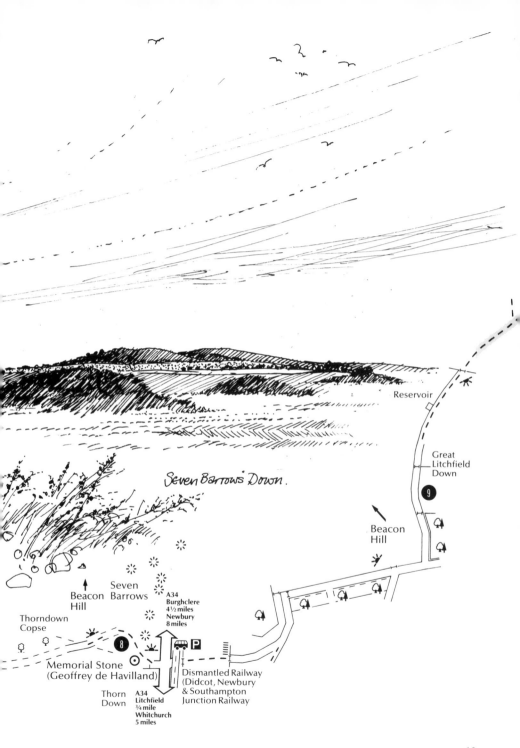

Reservoir

Great
Litchfield
Down

9

Seven Barrows Down.

Beacon
Hill

Seven
Barrows

Beacon
Hill

A34
Burghclere
4½ miles
Newbury
8 miles

Thorndown
Copse

8

P

Memorial Stone
(Geoffrey de Havilland)

Dismantled Railway
(Didcot, Newbury
& Southampton
Junction Railway

Thorn
Down

A34
Litchfield
¾ mile
Whitchurch
5 miles

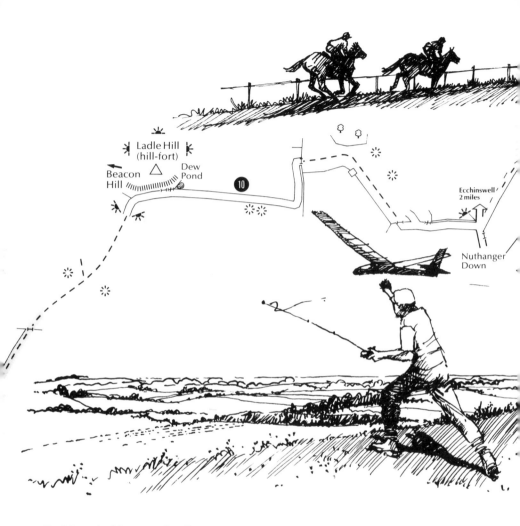

Ladle Hill
(hill-fort)

Beacon
Hill

Dew
Pond

10

Ecchinswell
2 miles

Nuthanger
Down

Prehistoric Man on the Downs

Ancient barrows and hill-forts will be visible at several places along the crest of the Downs, evidence that prehistoric man managed to feed, clothe, house and defend himself here and also developed social and religious beliefs that governed his activity. In Neolithic times (up to about 2000 BC) massive long earthen barrows were built for the collective burial of possibly 'upper class' people. Newcomers, arriving around 2000 BC, preferred single burials in smaller round barrows with the body usually in a crouched position and sometimes accompanied by a beaker made of pottery (hence 'the Beaker People').

In the 550 years before the birth of Christ — the period known as the Iron Age — there were successive invasions of tribes from the Continent. They brought new ideas and customs with them, and over the years advances were made in

Race horse training - Watership Down.

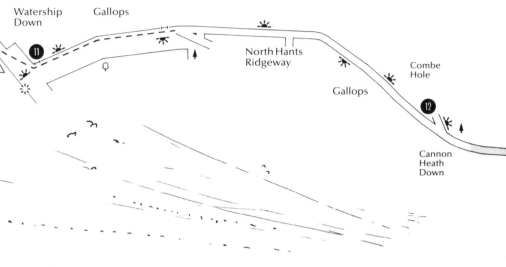

Watership Down

Gallops

North Hants Ridgeway

Combe Hole

Gallops

Cannon Heath Down

View from Iron age fort, 'Ladle' Hill.

Ladle Hill

On top of Ladle Hill is an early Iron Age hill-fort, possibly built as a defence against invaders, though an embanked enclosure to pen cattle in winter may have existed earlier. The fort, because unfinished, gives us some idea of how these massive earthworks were constructed. The line of the ditch was marked out, then dug by separate gangs working in different places. Large chalk blocks were used to prevent the rampart, built up from loose earth and chalk, falling back into the ditch. Ladle Hill and nearby Beacon Hill (whose hill-fort dates from the same time) defended an important route north — the forerunner of today's A34.

farming, defence and domestic life. Iron implements in use during the period included bill-hooks, sickles, saws, files, adzes, bolts and nails, while weaponry included iron daggers, swords, knives and spears. Money, at first in the form of iron currency bars, began to take the place of barter and overseas trade increased. Hill-forts continued to be built, and some may have served as political administrative centres for local chiefs.

21

The Downs at Kingsclere

The northern section of the Wayfarer's Walk is on the North Hants Ridgeway, a prehistoric track on a high chalk ridge through the North Hampshire Downs. The track can be followed from Basingstoke to the Vale of Pewsey in Wiltshire where it joins the Great Ridgeway. Chalk, made up of very small grains of calcium carbonate, is extremely porous. This makes an ideal surface for walkers and it grows ideal turf for racing horses — hence the gallops at White Hill where horses are trained and exercised. In dry weather there is a spring in the turf and with rain it's never too wet under foot.

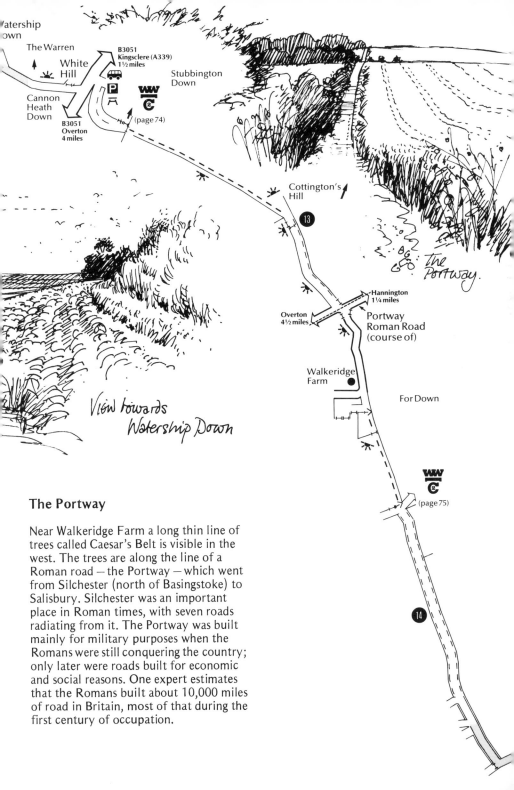

Watership Down

The Warren

White Hill

B3051 Kingsclere (A339) 1½ miles

Stubbington Down

Cannon Heath Down

B3051 Overton 4 miles

P

(page 74)

Cottington's Hill

13

The Portway

Hannington 1¼ miles

Overton 4½ miles

Portway Roman Road (course of)

Walkeridge Farm

For Down

View towards Watership Down

(page 75)

14

The Portway

Near Walkeridge Farm a long thin line of trees called Caesar's Belt is visible in the west. The trees are along the line of a Roman road – the Portway – which went from Silchester (north of Basingstoke) to Salisbury. Silchester was an important place in Roman times, with seven roads radiating from it. The Portway was built mainly for military purposes when the Romans were still conquering the country; only later were roads built for economic and social reasons. One expert estimates that the Romans built about 10,000 miles of road in Britain, most of that during the first century of occupation.

Warren Hill
Cottages

The
Manor
Farm

Overton
3¼ miles

Hannington
1 mile

**North
Oakley**

Pit

15

Freemantle
Farm

Freemantle Farm.

Farming

This is North Hampshire's cereal belt, the predominant crop being barley which grows well on chalk. Barley now accounts for about 30 per cent of the County's total area under crops and grass. It is usually planted in October and harvested in August. Brewing has been a traditional Hampshire industry — there were over 80 breweries in 1900; there are fewer than 10 today.

The observant walker will notice that a section of Great Deane Wood, marked on the O.S. map, no longer exists. Much

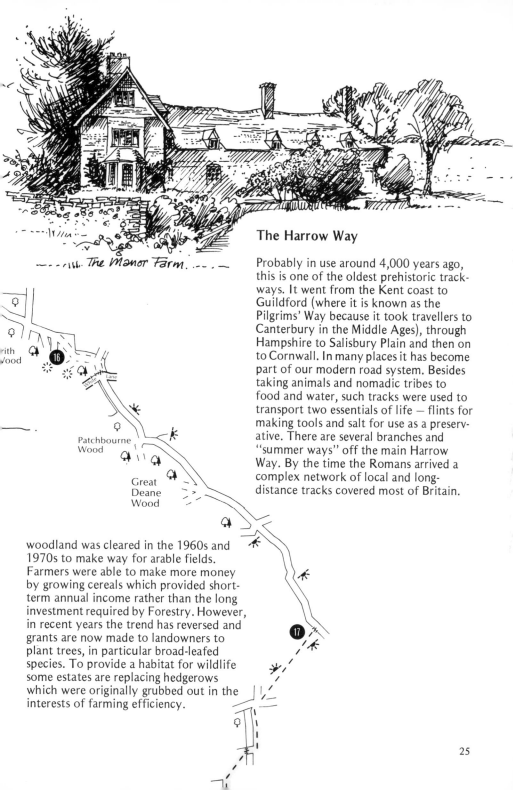

The Manor Farm

The Harrow Way

Probably in use around 4,000 years ago, this is one of the oldest prehistoric trackways. It went from the Kent coast to Guildford (where it is known as the Pilgrims' Way because it took travellers to Canterbury in the Middle Ages), through Hampshire to Salisbury Plain and then on to Cornwall. In many places it has become part of our modern road system. Besides taking animals and nomadic tribes to food and water, such tracks were used to transport two essentials of life — flints for making tools and salt for use as a preservative. There are several branches and "summer ways" off the main Harrow Way. By the time the Romans arrived a complex network of local and long-distance tracks covered most of Britain.

woodland was cleared in the 1960s and 1970s to make way for arable fields. Farmers were able to make more money by growing cereals which provided short-term annual income rather than the long investment required by Forestry. However, in recent years the trend has reversed and grants are now made to landowners to plant trees, in particular broad-leafed species. To provide a habitat for wildlife some estates are replacing hedgerows which were originally grubbed out in the interests of farming efficiency.

rith Wood

White Lane

Patchbourne Wood

Great Deane Wood

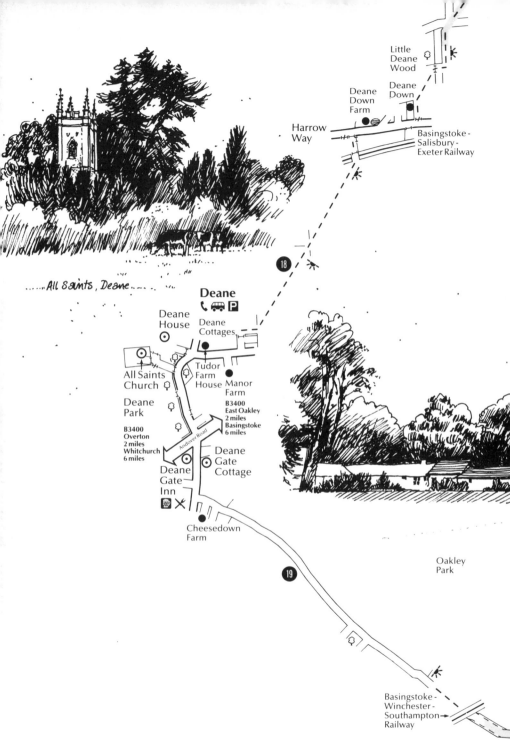

All Saints, Deane

Deane

☎ 🚌 🅿

Deane House ⊙

Deane Cottages ●

All Saints Church ♀

Tudor Farm House ♀

Manor Farm ●

Deane Park

B3400
Overton
2 miles
Whitchurch
6 miles

B3400
East Oakley
2 miles
Basingstoke
6 miles

Andover Road

Deane Gate Cottage ⊙ ●

Deane Gate Inn 🍴

Cheesedown Farm ●

Harrow Way

Little Deane Wood ♀

Deane Down Farm

Deane Down

Basingstoke - Salisbury - Exeter Railway

Oakley Park

Basingstoke - Winchester - Southampton Railway

18

19

Deane Gate Cottage and Inn.

Deane House

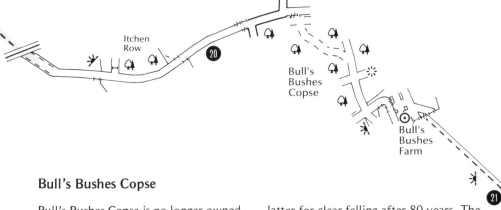

Bull's Bushes Copse

Bull's Bushes Copse is no longer owned by the Forestry Commission. Public access is now restricted to the public footpath through the Copse. The woodland consists of Douglas fir and beech, the former planted as an intermediate crop and the latter for clear-felling after 80 years. The trees were planted in 1954 in alternative strips three trees wide. The fir is being progressively removed in entire rows, while the beech is selectively thinned leaving the best trees to grow to maturity.

Bull's Bushes Farm.

Kempshott Park

The estate illustrates how financial pressures have altered the uses made of large stately homes and their grounds. At Kempshott, for example, the extensive grounds have been redeveloped as a golf course.

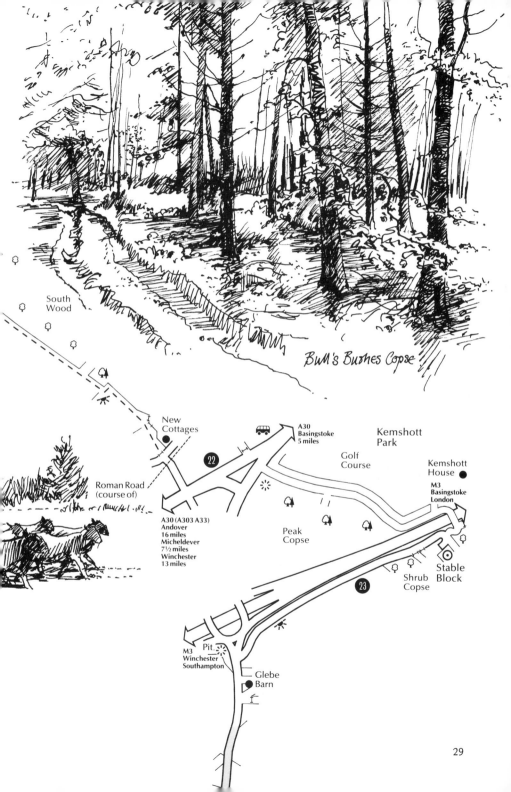

South
Wood

Bull's Bushes Copse

New
Cottages

Roman Road
(course of)

A30 (A303 A33)
Andover
16 miles
Micheldever
7½ miles
Winchester
13 miles

22

A30
Basingstoke
5 miles

Peak
Copse

Kemshott
Park

Golf
Course

Kemshott
House

M3
Basingstoke
London

23

Shrub
Copse

Stable
Block

M3
Winchester
Southampton

Pit

Glebe
Barn

View towards Dummer

The Queen Inn
Real Ales   Free House

All Saints Church

Well House &
Wheel

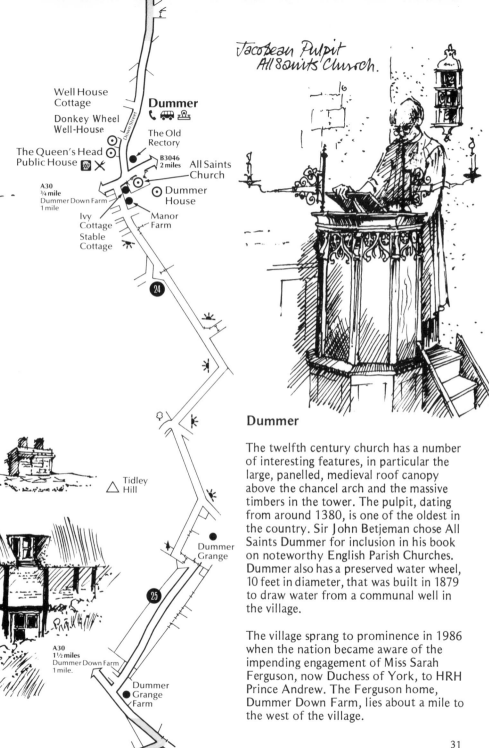

Well House
Cottage

Donkey Wheel
Well-House

The Queen's Head
Public House

A30
¾ mile
Dummer Down Farm
1 mile

Down Street

Dummer

The Old
Rectory

B3046
2 miles

All Saints
Church

Dummer
House

Ivy
Cottage

Manor
Farm

Stable
Cottage

24

Tidley
Hill

Dummer
Grange

25

A30
1½ miles
Dummer Down Farm
1 mile.

Dummer
Grange
Farm

*Jacobean Pulpit
All Saints Church.*

Dummer

The twelfth century church has a number
of interesting features, in particular the
large, panelled, medieval roof canopy
above the chancel arch and the massive
timbers in the tower. The pulpit, dating
from around 1380, is one of the oldest in
the country. Sir John Betjeman chose All
Saints Dummer for inclusion in his book
on noteworthy English Parish Churches.
Dummer also has a preserved water wheel,
10 feet in diameter, that was built in 1879
to draw water from a communal well in
the village.

The village sprang to prominence in 1986
when the nation became aware of the
impending engagement of Miss Sarah
Ferguson, now Duchess of York, to HRH
Prince Andrew. The Ferguson home,
Dummer Down Farm, lies about a mile to
the west of the village.

31

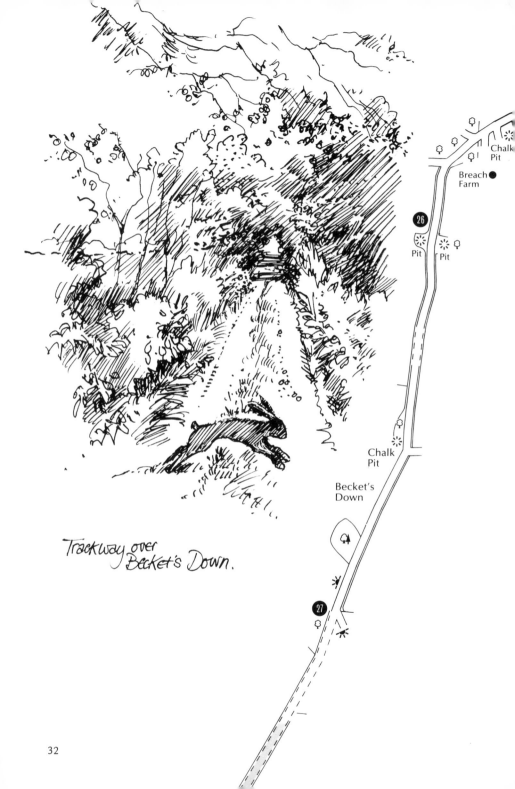

Trackway over Becket's Down.

Chalk Pit

Breach ● Farm

26

Pit ☀ ☀ Pit

Chalk Pit

Becket's Down

27

32

Breach
Cottages

Axford (B3046)
1½ miles

Old Chalk Pit on
Becket's Down.
(Reconstruction)

Chalk

The area between Becket's Down and
Dummer and around the A33 is dotted
with old chalk pits. Some of these are
now ploughed and grow crops but others
— like the one on the Wayfarer's Walk
north of Dummer Grange — have naturally
regenerated the oaks and beeches that
originally covered much of this area.
Chalk used to be dug out of the ground
for a variety of uses. Lime was made from
it, sometimes in kilns dug into the chalk
pits. It was also ground up very fine and
used as a whitener and for making paint,
putty, plaster and linoleum, and for hundreds of years it was used to fertilise the
soil, a process known as marling. An 1813
report on the state of farming in Hampshire for the Board of Agriculture and
Internal Improvement noted that: "There
is a very common opinion amongst most
improvers with chalk, that the deeper the
chalk is procured, the better it answers
the purposes for manure, from its falling
more readily to powder by exposure to
the air".

The Candovers

In late Saxon times the villages of Brown, Chilton and Preston Candover were small valley settlements surrounded by forest and grazing land. In the Middle Ages the land was owned by various lords of the manor and worked by the peasants who were allotted strips from the huge fields that surrounded the village. Later, as the ideas of the agricultural improvers took hold, some enclosure and reorganisation of land holdings occurred. But it was the 1823 Enclosure Award which drastically altered the landscape and people's social and economic position. Today this area consists mainly of farms that grow cereals (wheat and barley) and run dairy herds.

St. Peter's Church
Brown Candover

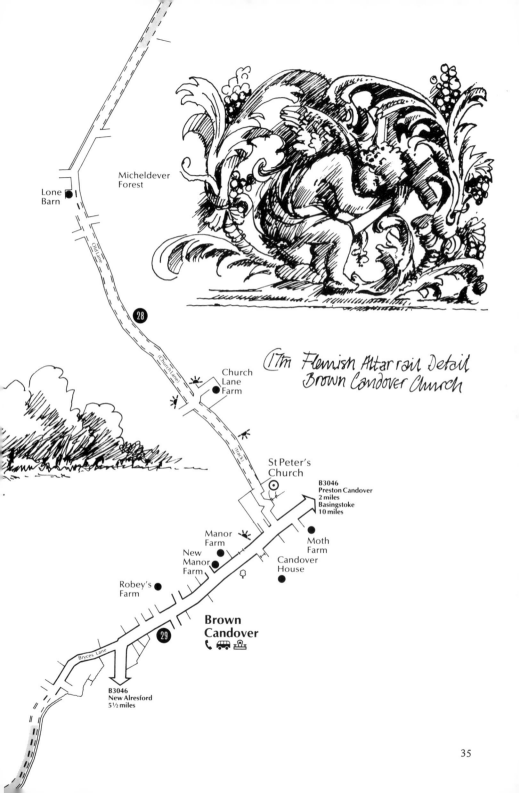

Lone
Barn

Micheldever
Forest

Old Lane

(28)

(Church Lane)

Church
Lane
Farm

(track)

17m Flemish Altar rail Detail
Brown Candover Church

St Peter's
Church

B3046
Preston Candover
2 miles
Basingstoke
10 miles

Manor
Farm

New
Manor
Farm

Moth
Farm

Candover
House

Robey's
Farm

**Brown
Candover**

(29)

Bryces Lane

B3046
New Alresford
5½ miles

35

The Lunway and Ox Drove

The Wayfarer's Walk follows a track known locally as the Ox Drove, though it is part of a very old cross-country route called the Lunway. The name Lunway appears in two Saxon charters and probably meant a popular track over the downs (lun = common place, dun = down). Later the name was given to a series of roughly connecting tracks of prehistoric, Saxon and medieval origins — tracks that developed in response to the need for defence, local and long-distance trade and droveways for cattle and sheep.

Totford Farm

There are numerous theories about the precise route, but it is safe to say that it went from Old Sarum to Stockbridge and Crawley, then north of Winchester, joining the Harrow Way east of Basingstoke. It stays mainly on the higher chalkland, avoiding steep ascents or descents where possible. Some parts of the supposed route may be deviations called 'summerways', used during better weather when the going was easier. Some of the route is incorporated into today's road system, for example, the A30 from the Wiltshire border to Stockbridge. At the Woolpack sheep were penned in nearby fields while tne drovers drank and slept the night away before heading to Farnham market.

The Woolpack Inn.

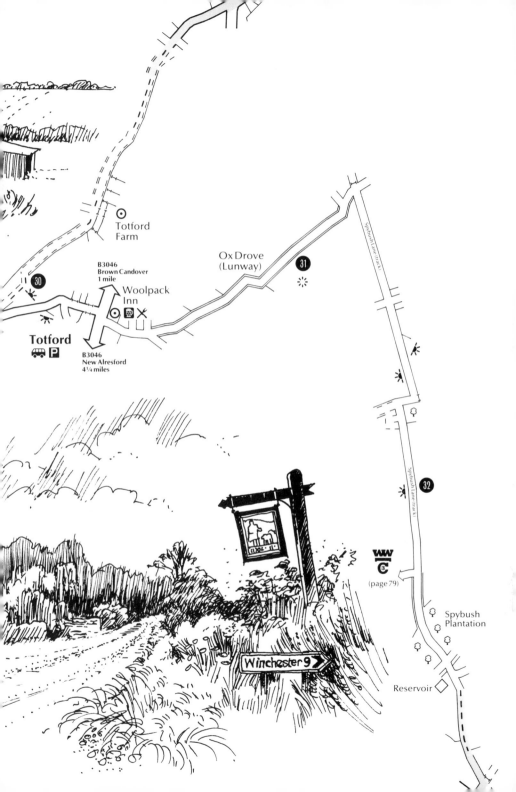

Totford
Farm

B3046
Brown Candover
1 mile

Ox Drove
(Lunway)

30

31

**Woolpack
Inn**

Totford

B3046
New Alresford
4¼ miles

Spybush Lane (track)

Spybush Lane (track)

32

(page 79)

Spybush
Plantation

Reservoir

Winchester 9

Abbotstone Farm & Earthworks

Abbotstone Down

32.25 acres at Abbotstone Down were purchased by the County Council and are now managed as natural downland and scrub, and kept as open space for recreational purposes. Many types of downland flora and fauna thrive up here, surrounded by a sea of intensively farmed land. Oliver's Battery was an Iron Age hill-fort, now much reduced in size. There is no evidence that it was used during the Civil War and other forts in Hampshire have the same name (at Winchester and Basingstoke, for example), probably to commemorate the fighting of 1644.

Abbotstone (Lost Village)

Near the Candover Stream at Abbotstone is the site of a deserted village that once covered 15 acres. Besides the evidence on the ground — earthworks, depressions, a graveyard — it is known that 18 parishioners were wealthy enough to be taxed in 1327 and that a 100-room mansion was being built in 1719 — "a noble brick house edged with stone" is a contemporary description, but no more is known about it.

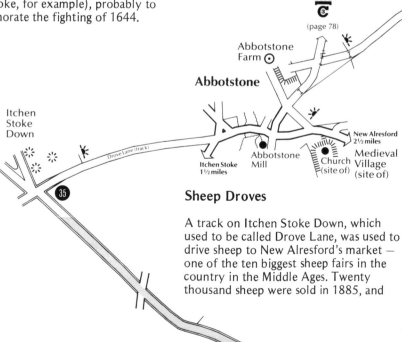

(page 78)

Sheep Droves

A track on Itchen Stoke Down, which used to be called Drove Lane, was used to drive sheep to New Alresford's market — one of the ten biggest sheep fairs in the country in the Middle Ages. Twenty thousand sheep were sold in 1885, and

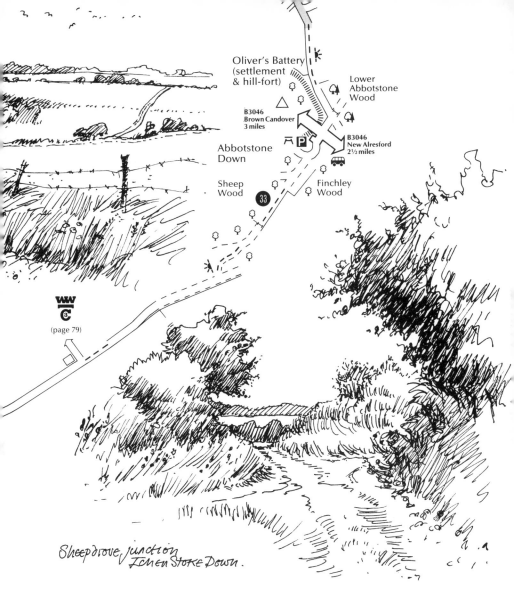

10,000 were still being brought to market here in 1937, but the fair died out in the 1970's. Note the intersection where five old trackways meet next to some tumuli. In the Middle Ages the landscape here would have looked very different, the tracks winding through rough open downland with scrub and trees in places. The hedgerows and trees around Itchen Stoke Down were probably planted a few hundred years ago when land was enclosed for sheep walks.

New Alresford *Fulling Mill*

The railway between Alton and Winchester — the Mid-Hants 'Watercress Line' — was opened in 1865 and closed by British Rail in 1973. In its day it carried freight, passengers and troop trains, as well as taking from New Alresford station enough locally grown watercress to supply most of the country. Eight or nine tons would often leave here daily at the height of the season. The line between Ropley and New Alresford was re-opened as a steam railway in 1977 by a private company with much help from the Mid-Hants Railway Preservation Society. Since then it has been extended to Alton where it connects with the British Rail line at Alton Station.

The T-shaped plan of New Alresford was laid out by Godfrey de Lucy, Bishop of Winchester, at the end of the 12th century. He created a thriving market at Broad Street (once called Market Place) as well as making New Alresford a major centre for the wool industry. He built the Great Weir, the associated sluices and Alresford Pond (now reduced from its original 200

acres to about 60), a great achievement for the time. Writing about it 85 years later, one commentator said: "Now in 1189 Godfrey de Lucy ... formed a noble and magnificent plan for improving the trade of both Winchester and Alresford by the establishment of a navigation on the River Alre or Itchen, which stupendous work he is said to have undertaken at his own expense"

The reason for so much elegant Georgian architecture in a town that was prosperous hundreds of years before the 18th century is that fires did a great deal of damage in 1440, 1610 and 1620. Then, in 1679, a really terrible fire devastated the whole town, destroying most of the timber-framed buildings in a few hours. West Street suffered another fire in 1736.

Broad Street.

River Alre

There is a lovely stretch along the peaceful, tree-lined River Alre. Keep an eye out for watercress beds and watch trout through the crystal clear waters. At the fulling mill, over 300 years old, homespun wool was scoured, washed, pounded with feet or mallets, stretched, dried, brushed and sheared.

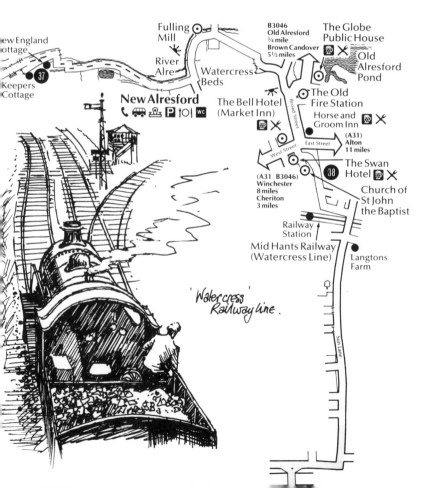

Fulling Mill

ew England ottage

River Alre

Keepers Cottage

37

Watercress Beds

New Alresford

The Bell Hotel (Market Inn)

West Street

(A31 B3046) Winchester 8 miles Cheriton 3 miles

B3046 Old Alresford ¼ mile Brown Candover 5½ miles

The Globe Public House

Old Alresford Pond

The Old Fire Station

Horse and Groom Inn

Broad Street

East Street

(A31) Alton 11 miles

38

The Swan Hotel

Church of St John the Baptist

Railway Station

Mid Hants Railway (Watercress Line)

Langtons Farm

Sun Lane

'Watercress' Railway line.

41

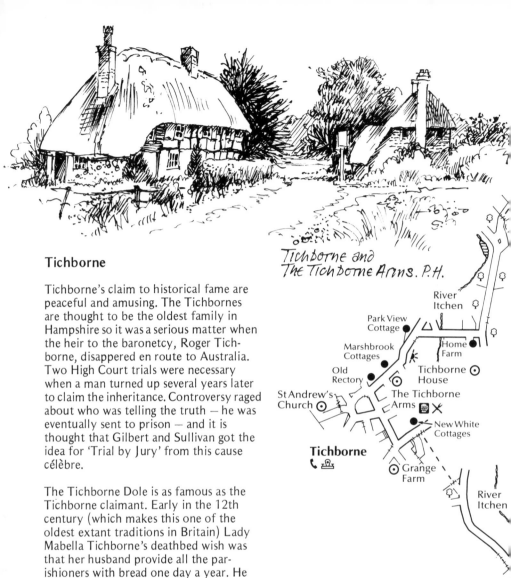

Tichborne

Tichborne's claim to historical fame are peaceful and amusing. The Tichbornes are thought to be the oldest family in Hampshire so it was a serious matter when the heir to the baronetcy, Roger Tichborne, disappered en route to Australia. Two High Court trials were necessary when a man turned up several years later to claim the inheritance. Controversy raged about who was telling the truth – he was eventually sent to prison – and it is thought that Gilbert and Sullivan got the idea for 'Trial by Jury' from this cause célèbre.

The Tichborne Dole is as famous as the Tichborne claimant. Early in the 12th century (which makes this one of the oldest extant traditions in Britain) Lady Mabella Tichborne's deathbed wish was that her husband provide all the parishioners with bread one day a year. He promised to give them all the flour from the land she could crawl around while a torch continued to burn. According to tradition she managed to get around 23 acres. He kept his promise and to this day every parishioner in Tichborne and Cheriton receives a gallon of flour (half-gallons for children) on Lady Day. It is thought that Cheriton Mill was used to grind flour from 'The Crawls', as the field is still known.

The avenue of trees to the east of Tichborne Park was planted between 70 and 100 years ago, and comprises mainly lime with some horse chestnut, ash, oak, beech and sycamore. Lime trees, with their graceful upright form, were often used to adorn the front drives of country houses.

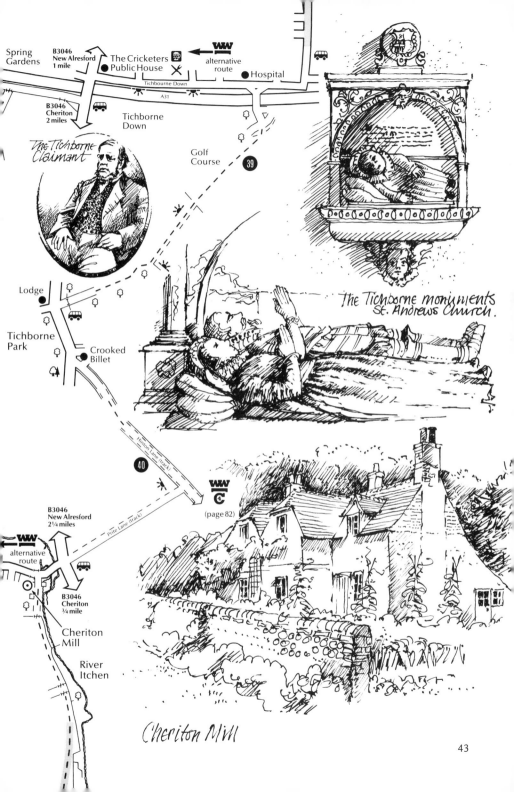

Spring
Gardens

B3046
New Alresford
1 mile

The Cricketers
Public House

alternative
route

Hospital

Tichbourne Down

A31

B3046
Cheriton
2 miles

Tichborne
Down

*The Tichborne
Claimant*

Golf
Course

39

*The Tichborne monuments
St. Andrews Church.*

Lodge

Tichborne
Park

Crooked
Billet

Hinton Lane (track)

40

B3046
New Alresford
2¼ miles

alternative
route

(page 82)

Prite Lane (track)

B3046
Cheriton
¾ mile

Cheriton
Mill

River
Itchen

Cheriton Mill

Cheriton

With a wealth of vernacular architecture, the sparkling River Itchen winding through the village green, ducks wandering nearby, and the church sitting atop a prehistoric barrow, it is not surprising that Cheriton oftens wins Hampshire's Best Kept Village competition. There are water meadows to the north of the village — providing a good habitat for wetland flora — and to the east is a network of very old tracks and lanes, perhaps made in the Middle Ages to provide access to common fields and to take sheep to Alresford market. Today their thick hedgerows provide habitat for a variety of birds and small animals.

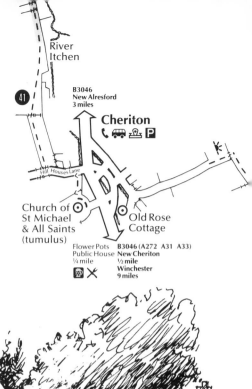

River Itchen

B3046
New Alresford
3 miles

41

Cheriton

Hill Houses Lane

Church of
St Michael
& All Saints
(tumulus)

Old Rose
Cottage

Flower Pots   B3046 (A272 A31 A33)
Public House   New Cheriton
¼ mile   ½ mile
                 Winchester
                 9 miles

Old Rose Cottage - Cheriton.

Hinton Ampner

Much thought was given to tree planting on the slopes above Hinton Ampner House as the owner found the southern view from the house bleak and barren. The result is two large plantations of mixed trees, especially chestnut, beech and Norway maple. The east-west track that is crossed to the south of the grounds of the house is thought to be the old coaching road from Winchester to Petersfield, formerly called Mud Lane or Water Lane. The source of the River Itchen is less than half a mile west of here.

The village of Hinton Ampner appears unaffected by the passage of time. The Manor House, church and a few cottages sit peacefully in their well-wooded setting. Many of the trees — lime, horse and Spanish chestnut, Norway maple, Turkey oak — were planted by the last private owner whose family were connected with the Manor for over 300 years. On his death in 1986 the estate was left to the National Trust. The church dates from Saxon times, with a good deal of the original work surviving subsequent alterations.

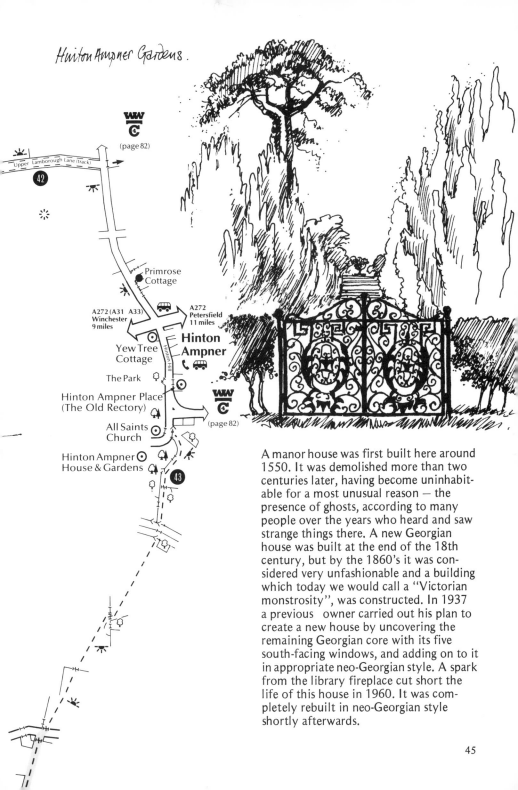

Hinton Ampner Gardens.

(page 82)

Upper Lamborough Lane (track)

42

Primrose Cottage

A272 (A31 A33)
Winchester
9 miles

A272
Petersfield
11 miles

Hinton Ampner

Yew Tree Cottage

Hinton Hill

The Park

Hinton Ampner Place
(The Old Rectory)

All Saints
Church

(page 82)

Hinton Ampner
House & Gardens

43

A manor house was first built here around 1550. It was demolished more than two centuries later, having become uninhabitable for a most unusual reason — the presence of ghosts, according to many people over the years who heard and saw strange things there. A new Georgian house was built at the end of the 18th century, but by the 1860's it was considered very unfashionable and a building which today we would call a "Victorian monstrosity", was constructed. In 1937 a previous owner carried out his plan to create a new house by uncovering the remaining Georgian core with its five south-facing windows, and adding on to it in appropriate neo-Georgian style. A spark from the library fireplace cut short the life of this house in 1960. It was completely rebuilt in neo-Georgian style shortly afterwards.

45

St Andrews Church

Kilmeston Manor

South Hants Ridgeway

The South Hants Ridgeway is a prehistoric
track that probably went from Kent to
Salisbury Plain, where it then joined several
tracks that went to the west country and
south coast seaports. The route is not
always clear on the ground today.

The best known section where the route
is certain is on the chalk uplands through
East and West Sussex. The Countryside
Commission's proposals for an extension
of the South Downs Way to Winchester
includes the track from Wind Farm,
through Lomer, to Beacon Hill overlook-
ing the Meon Valley. The hedgerow near
Lomer coincides with an old boundary
hedge and contains about eleven different
tree and shrub species, an indication that
it may have existed for around 1,000 years.

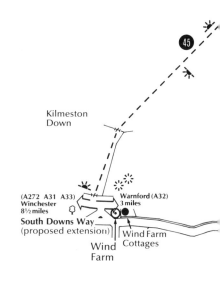

Kilmeston
Down

(A272 A31 A33)
Winchester
8½ miles

Warnford (A32)
3 miles

South Downs Way
(proposed extension)

Wind Farm
Cottages

Wind
Farm

46

Kilmeston ⊙
Manor
New Cheriton (A272)
1 mile
St Andrew's
Church

Kilmeston
📞 🚌

Dean
House
⊙

44

Wind Farm

From the ridge at Wind Farm there is a panoramic view of spacious arable fields, hedge-lined lanes, low hills and occasional woodland stretching north to Cheriton and New Alresford. This is very much chalk country, though there are caps of clay over the chalk in places.

Warnford
Plantation

South Hants
Ridgeway

46

View north from ridge at Wind Farm

47

Preshaw Down
from Betty Mundy's Bottom

Betty Mundy's Bottom

Norway spruce and Corsican pine are
planted on the track south of Betty
Mundy's Bottom. (According to local
legend Betty Mundy was a lady of dubious
reputation who lured travellers to her
cottage with promises of enjoyment. She
then stole their possessions, murdered
them and put them down the well). It
will be noticeable around Preshaw Wood
that many trees have been felled in recent
years and the cleared land reclaimed for
agricultural use. This has meant a loss of
wildlife habitats. Rabbit Copse was planted
in the 1940's with a mixture of broad-
leaved and coniferous species. Most of the
softwood has been removed, leaving a
final crop of ash, sycamore and oak.

Lomer

From the Wayfarer's Walk you can look
east across a field towards the site of the
deserted medieval village of Lomer which
is a protected scheduled Ancient Monument. Bad harvests and plagues, including
the Black Death which depopulated much
of the countryside, probably caused
Lomer's disappearance at the end of the
14th century. Archaeologists have found
indications on the ground of the major
house and other homesteads.

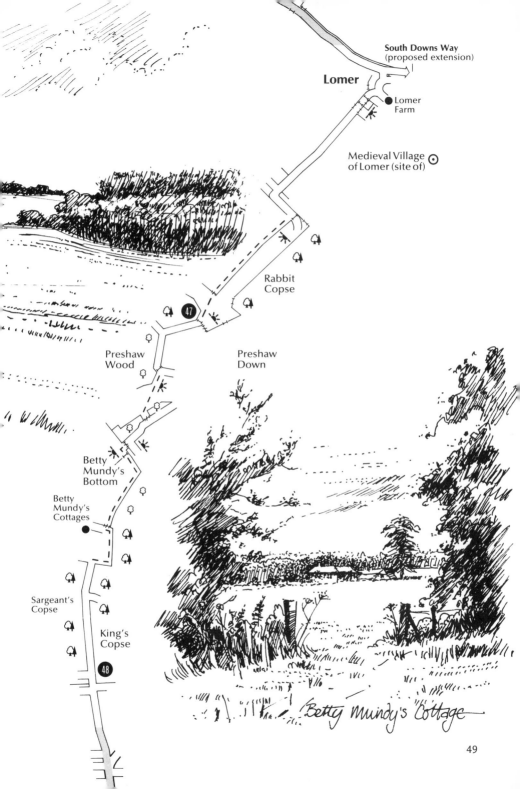

South Downs Way
(proposed extension)

Lomer

Lomer
Farm

Medieval Village ⊙
of Lomer (site of)

Rabbit
Copse

47

Preshaw
Wood

Preshaw
Down

Betty
Mundy's
Bottom

Betty
Mundy's
Cottages

Sargeant's
Copse

King's
Copse

48

Betty Mundy's Cottage

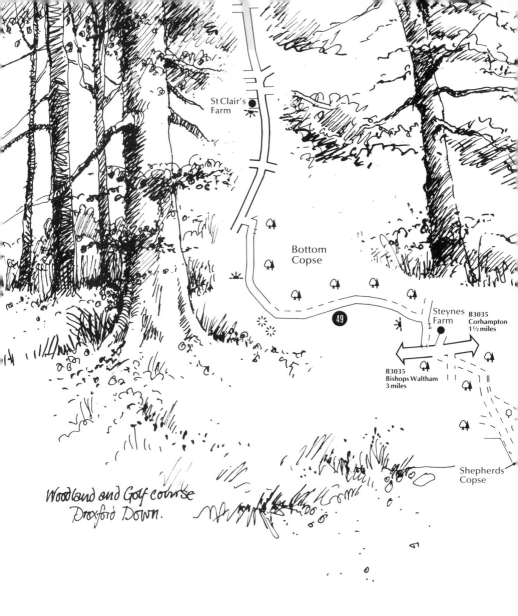

St Clair's Farm

Bottom Copse

49

Steynes Farm

B3035
Corhampton
1½ miles

B3035
Bishops Waltham
3 miles

Shepherds Copse

Woodland and Golf course
Droxford Down.

Woodlands

This is the most wooded section of the
Wayfarer's Walk. The route goes through
a coppiced hazel wood, a larch plantation
(with older oak and beech standards left
in places) and an old beech wood. Bottom
Copse is a mixture of beech and fir trees.

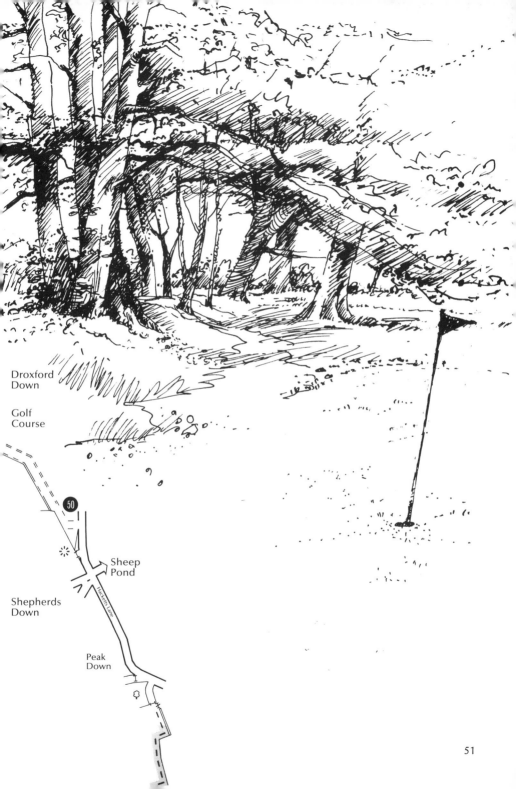

Droxford
Down

Golf
Course

50

Sheep
Pond

Shepherds
Down

Hacketts Lane

Peak
Down

51

grew up, with each man cultivating his own strips of land in huge communal fields as well as doing some work for the lord of the manor. The isolated farmsteads south of the Wayfarer's Walk near Hambledon (Broom Farm, Hoe Cross Farm, Russels's Farm) indicate that separate enclosures were later cleared from the forest, perhaps by industrious farmers in the 17th century.

The Wayfarer's Walk passes Soberton church, described by Sir Nikolaus Pevsner as "a puzzle church, if ever there was one". One of its more unusual features is the carving on the tower of a man's head with a key and a woman's head with a pail, presumably to commemorate the generous

Church of St Mary & all Saints Droxford.

River Meon.

St Peter's Church Soberton.

Meon Valley

The Wayfarer's Walk goes through two of the peaceful villages beside the river. Although there is some evidence of Bronze Age, Iron Age and Roman settlement in the area, the first big impact on the valley was made by a tribe of Jutes called the Meonwara which populated the valley after the Anglo-Saxon invasion of the coast. The heavier clay soil that extends north from the coast changes, in the parish of Soberton, to the chalk belt that runs far to the north. On the chalk soil the trees and undergrowth were less dense and therefore easier to clear. As the population increased over the years villages

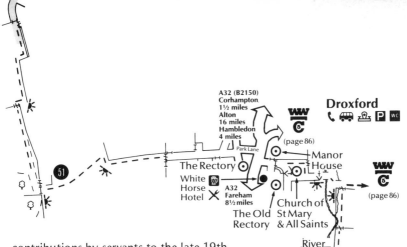

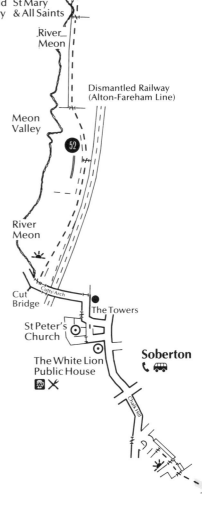

contributions by servants to the late 19th century restoration of the church. The walk between Soberton and Droxford is alongside the river and through a horse chestnut copse, with water meadows and a beech-studded hillside on one side, a railway embankment on the other. The Meon Valley line connected Alton to Fareham. It was built in 1903, quite late for the building of new railways, but was closed in stages during the 1950's and '60's. Its moment of glory was at Droxford station where, from 2-4 June 1944, the War Cabinet and the allied chiefs waited for the right moment to launch the invasion of Europe.

Droxford means "ford at the dry place", and as at Warnford farther up the Meon Valley it was here possible for the Saxon invaders to cross the river. Picture then Izaak Walton, over a thousand years later, fishing peacefully in the Meon at Droxford (his daughter had married the rector), and thinking that this valley "exceeds all England for swift, shallow, clear, pleasant brooks and store of trout". There are many attractive Georgian houses in the village which use local roofing tiles and there is an abundance of the lovely grey bricks patterned with red. Shepherd's Down, a mile to the north of Droxford, with Sheep Pond nearby, was probably a resting place for shepherds and sheep on their way to the huge market at New Alresford.

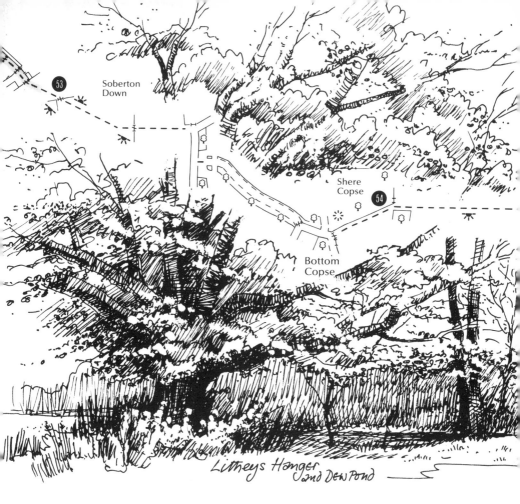

Soberton
Down

53

Shere
Copse

54

Bottom
Copse

Litheys Hanger
and Dew Pond

Hambledon

Hambledon nestles in the floor of a gentle valley, surrounded by wooded hillsides that provide a vivid display of autumn colours. There is evidence of some Iron Age and Roman occupation in the vicinity. The Saxons, in the 11th century, built a small stone church, a great deal of which remains inside the "new" church built in the following centuries. William the Conqueror seized the church's land, but it was later returned to the Bishop of Winchester who was granted a weekly market at Hambledon in the 13th century. As a

"town" with its own market Hambledon grew rapidly, and the church was enlarged several times during the 13th century. The town prospered in the Middle Ages, but in the 19th century Hambledon's decline began. Cobbet noted that it was "partaking in the fate of all those places which were formerly a sort of rendezvous for persons who had things to buy and things to sell". Today a grocery called 'The People's Market' is a reminder of Hambledon's past.

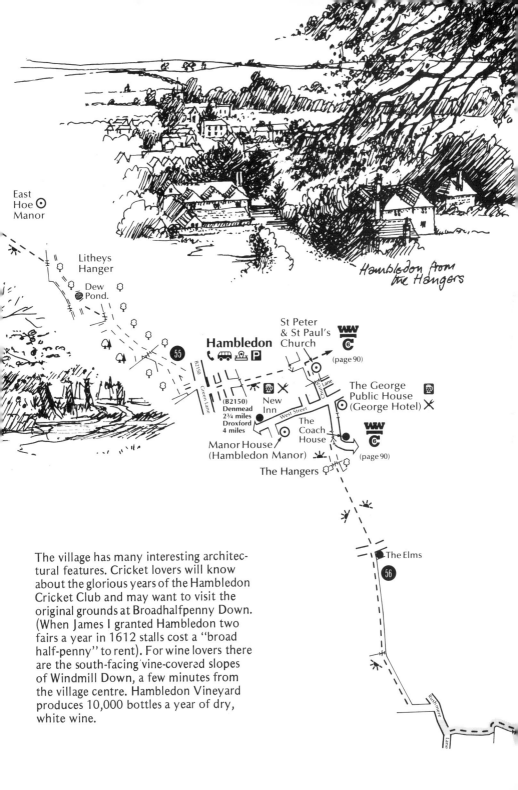

East
Hoe ◉
Manor

Litheys
Hanger

Dew
Pond.

St Peter
& St Paul's
Hambledon Church

55

The George
Public House
(George Hotel)

(page 90)

(B2150)
Denmead
2¾ miles
Droxford
4 miles

New
Inn

West Street

The
Coach
House

Manor House
(Hambledon Manor)

The Hangers

(page 90)

Hambledon from the Hangers

The Elms

56

Rushmere Lane

The village has many interesting architec-
tural features. Cricket lovers will know
about the glorious years of the Hambledon
Cricket Club and may want to visit the
original grounds at Broadhalfpenny Down.
(When James I granted Hambledon two
fairs a year in 1612 stalls cost a "broad
half-penny" to rent). For wine lovers there
are the south-facing vine-covered slopes
of Windmill Down, a few minutes from
the village centre. Hambledon Vineyard
produces 10,000 bottles a year of dry,
white wine.

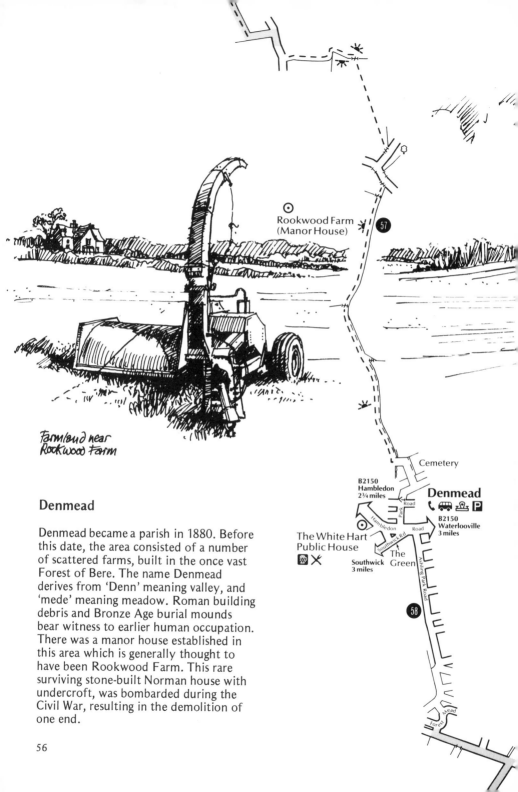

Rookwood Farm
(Manor House)   57

Farmland near
Rookwood Farm

Cemetery

B2150
Hambledon
2¾ miles

Denmead

The White Hart
Public House

B2150
Waterlooville
3 miles

Southwick
3 miles

The
Green

58

Denmead

Denmead became a parish in 1880. Before
this date, the area consisted of a number
of scattered farms, built in the once vast
Forest of Bere. The name Denmead
derives from 'Denn' meaning valley, and
'mede' meaning meadow. Roman building
debris and Bronze Age burial mounds
bear witness to earlier human occupation.
There was a manor house established in
this area which is generally thought to
have been Rookwood Farm. This rare
surviving stone-built Norman house with
undercroft, was bombarded during the
Civil War, resulting in the demolition of
one end.

The low coastline and natural harbours have made this area more vulnerable to invasion than almost any other place in Britain. As a result, "Nowhere else in England," says one authority on the subject, "is there such a concentration and variety of forts of so many periods". Carisbrooke Castle on the Isle of Wight was the first castle to be built with gunports in 1380. The first dry dock in England was built in Portsmouth by Henry VII in 1484. Sixty years later an earth rampart with towers was built and Portsmouth got its first cannon. The town and harbour were further fortified when Charles II started twenty years of building fortresses, and in the 18th century the whole of Portsea Island was supplied with fortifications.

Portsdown Hill has been a crucial communication link between Whitehall and the fleet at Portsmouth. In 1796 signals were sent via Portsdown using shutters and powerful fixed telescopes to read the signals. An improved system using semaphore was installed 30 years later. One of the stations was about a mile west of Bedhampton at a height of 250 feet on the east slope of Portsdown. It was demolished in 1861 to make way for Farlington Redoubt.

View over Portsmouth and Isle of Wight.

FORT PURBROOK

Golf Course

Fort Purbrook

...sdown Hill Road

63

Ports Down

Military Road

64

Portsdown Hill Road   B2177

Pit

Portsdown Hill

Just west of Bedhampton the route follows one of Hampshire's most interesting geological features — a narrow ridge of chalk which rises, steeply in places, from the coastal strip of clay and coarse sand and extends for six miles between Bedhampton and Fareham. As you walk along Portsdown Hill there are superb views of Portsmouth. Below lie the Naval Dockyard, now much reduced, the commercial port and Continental Ferry terminal, and the city itself edged by Portsmouth and Langstone Harbours. Beyond is Spithead with views to the Isle of Wight.

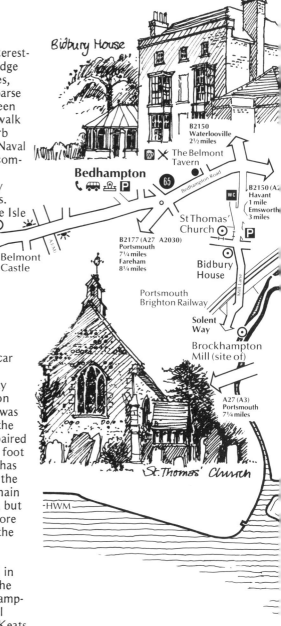

Bedhampton

The walker is far more aware of Bedhampton's existence than is the car driver, for whom it is merely part of Portsmouth's suburbs. The Domesday book records a church at Bedhampton and 25 families. The present church was built in the 12th century to replace the Saxon one, and was enlarged and repaired in the 14th and 19th centuries. The 11 foot wide chancel arch dating from 1140 has survived unscathed. Until the end of the 16th century sheep rearing was the main land use in Bedhampton and Havant, but during the 17th century more and more land was enclosed and ploughed for the production of corn. Corn mills soon followed, much flour was shipped to London, and Bedhampton prospered in the 18th century. A plaque records the visit of poet John Keats with a Bedhampton miller, John Snook of Lower Mill House: "In this house in 1819 John Keats finished his poem 'The Eve of St. Agnes' and here in 1820 he spent his last night in England". He died in Rome of consumption a few months later, age 26.

Langstone Harbour

At Langstone Harbour are the 18th century mill (now converted to a house) and the pub (licensed since 1727), that sit on the water's edge at Langstone. Before a causeway and road were constructed in 1824 people walked across to Hayling Island at low tide. Forty years later Havant and Hayling Island were linked by 4½ miles of railway, but the branch line closed in 1963. Over the years there have been several schemes to develop Langstone as a commercial port, but they never came to anything. Today it is a quiet oasis compared to Chichester, Portsmouth and Southampton harbours.

Langstone Harbour, with its saltmarsh islands, tidal creeks, sandbanks and mud-flats, covers almost 5,000 acres between Portsea and Hayling Islands. It is home for wintering fowl such as dark-bellied brent geese, shellduck and teal, and for waders such as oyster-catcher, grey plover, curlew and redshank. The Harbour's wild-life and biological importance are inter-nationally recognised, and it has been scheduled by the Nature Conservancy Council as a Site of Special Scientific Interest. Probably best known are the thousands of brent geese who come to Langstone from the Russian sub-arctic in October and stay until March. Black-necked grebe are also habitual winter visitors, as well as birds of prey such as hen harrier, peregrine falcon, merlin and short-eared owl. The Royal Society for the Protection of Birds owns 1370 acres in the northern part of Langstone Harbour.

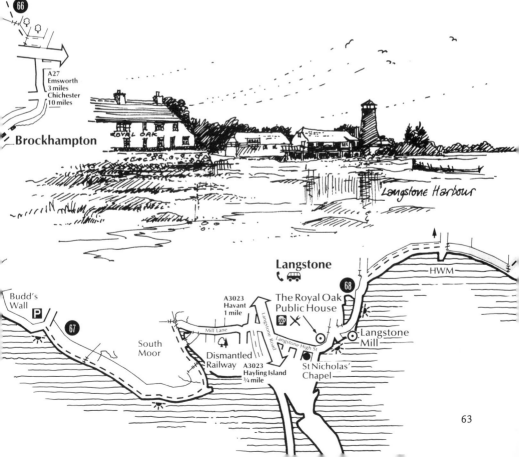

66

A27
Emsworth
3 miles
Chichester
10 miles

Brockhampton

Langstone Harbour

Langstone

HWM

Budd's
Wall
P

67

South
Moor

A3023
Havant
1 mile

Mill Lane

Langstone Road

The Royal Oak
Public House

68

Langstone High St

Langstone
Mill

Dismantled
Railway

A3023
Hayling Island
¾ mile

St Nicholas'
Chapel

Warblington Church

The two small flint buildings in the church yard are grave-watcher's huts, built about 200 years ago at a time when medical students were willing to pay handsome prices for corpses and thieves were willing to do the dirty work necessary to obtain them. The enormous yew tree, another striking feature in this churchyard, is thought to be somewhere between 600 and 900 years old. It was treated for decay about fifty years ago — note the cement filling — and has kept its majestic appearance.

Warblington Castle Farm.

Warblington Castle

The only remains of Warblington Castle is a tall octagonal red brick turret. Margaret, the Countess of Salisbury, was given lands at Warblington in 1513. The Castle, a large and imposing residence with four towers and a moat, was built for her over the next twelve years. It contained State apartments, a spacious hall, a private chapel and a great gallery. However, Margaret's friendship with Catherine of Aragon and her support for the Pope were too much for Henry. As a plaque on the turret tells us, she "lived in this Castle until she was executed at the Tower of London in 1541 by King Henry VIII".

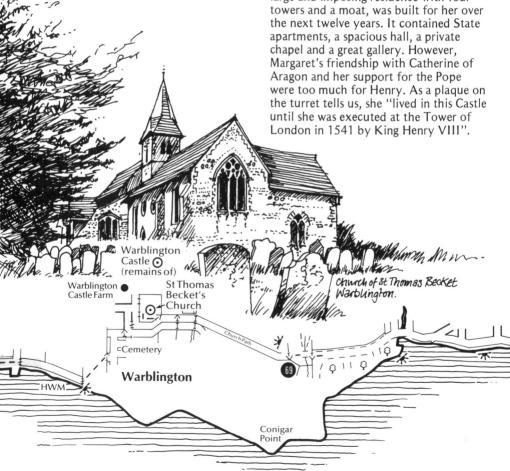

Church of St Thomas Becket Warblington.

Warblington Castle ⊙ (remains of)

Warblington Castle Farm ●

St Thomas Becket's Church

⊡ Cemetery

Church Path

Warblington

HWM

69

Conigar Point

64

Emsworth

The Wayfarer's Walk starts or finishes beside the yacht filled harbour of Emsworth, a small but bustling town on the tidal creek that divides Hampshire from Sussex. Emsworth has always been a lively place — corn milling, rope making, building small craft, fishing and particularly the oyster trade have all contributed to the town's prosperity in the past. Today it is an important centre for pleasure boating, with many yachts being wintered in the harbour. Fishing boats are still at work, however, and several boatyards still build yachts.

During the Middle Ages Emsworth began to grow at the expense of nearby Warblington. In the 13th century the right to hold a market was granted to Emsworth as Warblington was too close to the market at Havant. Later, during the Black Death, evacuees from Warblington were sent to Emsworth and in the 15th century less willing evacuees were moved there so that a private deer park could be created around Warblington. It was in the late 17th and early 18th centuries that Emsworth's fortune rose rapidly as the demand for food in London swelled. Hampshire farmers began to grow more corn, the streams and tides around Emsworth provided power for mills and large granaries soon sprang up. You can see a reminder of the thriving business as you walk around the quayside, for in the modern guise of the Emsworth Slipper Sailing Club is one of Emsworth's old tidal mills.

From the path around the coast there are fine views of Thorney and Hayling Islands, and of the mud-flats dotted with sails at most times of the year.

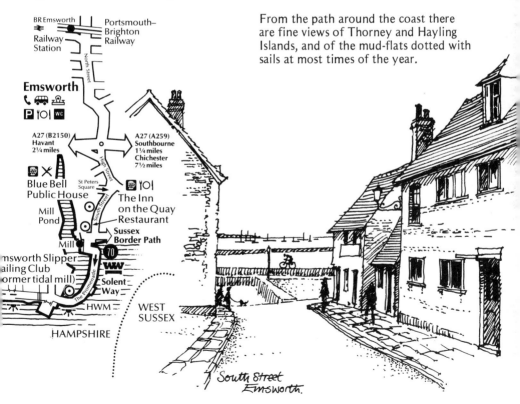

South Street
Emsworth.

View from Pict Hill

Wayfarers Walk
Circular routes

Trackway

Climb through leafy
tree-lined tracks to the high ground where
spectacular views are revealed over the
diminutive rural communities of East End
and East Woodhay. But the trackway has a
more ancient history. For centuries the
scarp was traversed by heavily constructed
wooden wagons hauled by lumbering
teams of oxen. It was the preferred winter
route, despite its severe exposure to the
seasonal gales, for its terrain was a firmer
alternative to the rutted muddy routes of
the valley below.

traverses airy scarp

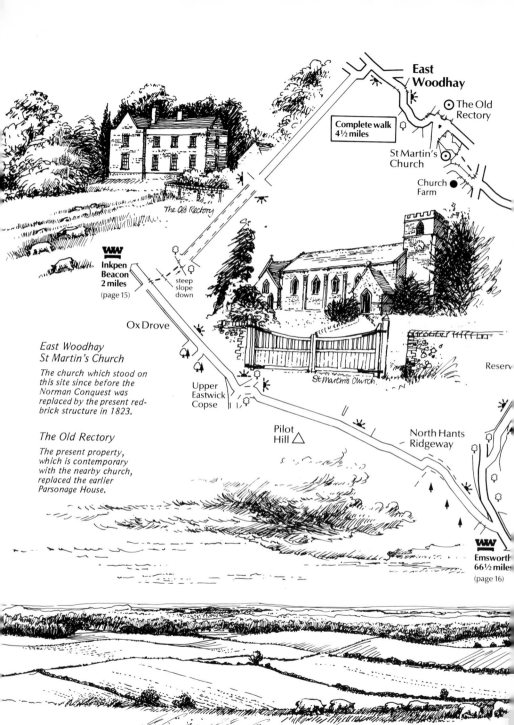

East Woodhay

The Old Rectory

Complete walk
4½ miles

St Martin's Church

Church Farm

⊙ The Old Rectory

St Martin's ⊙
Church

Church ●
Farm

Inkpen
Beacon
2 miles
(page 15)

steep
slope
down

Ox Drove

Upper
Eastwick
Copse

The Old Rectory

Reserv

St Martins Church

East Woodhay
St Martin's Church

The church which stood on this site since before the Norman Conquest was replaced by the present red-brick structure in 1823.

The Old Rectory

The present property, which is contemporary with the nearby church, replaced the earlier Parsonage House.

Pilot
Hill △

North Hants
Ridgeway

Emsworth
66½ miles
(page 16)

View near Pilot Hill

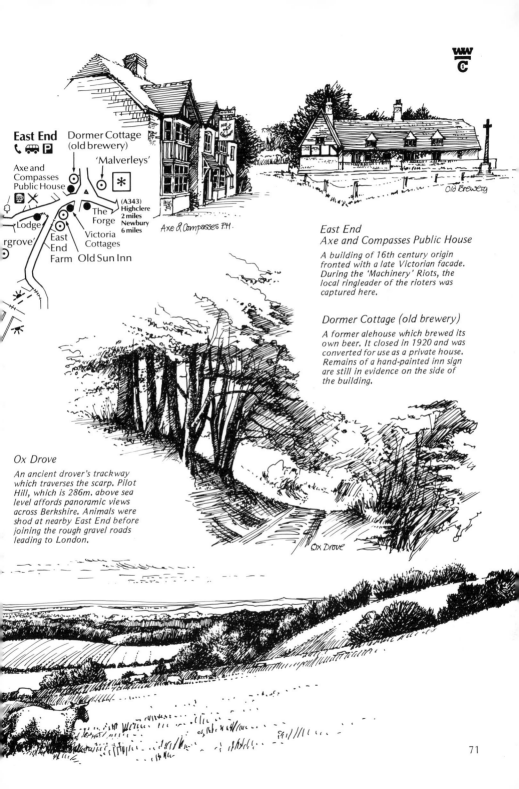

East End

☎ 🚌 🅿

Axe and
Compasses
Public House

Dormer Cottage
(old brewery)

'Malverleys'

✳

(A343)
Highclere
2 miles
Newbury
6 miles

The
Forge

'Lodge'

'rgrove'

East
End
Farm

Victoria
Cottages

Old Sun Inn

Axe & Compasses P.H.

Old Brewery

East End
Axe and Compasses Public House

A building of 16th century origin fronted with a late Victorian facade. During the 'Machinery' Riots, the local ringleader of the rioters was captured here.

Dormer Cottage (old brewery)

A former alehouse which brewed its own beer. It closed in 1920 and was converted for use as a private house. Remains of a hand-painted inn sign are still in evidence on the side of the building.

Ox Drove

An ancient drover's trackway which traverses the scarp. Pilot Hill, which is 286m. above sea level affords panoramic views across Berkshire. Animals were shod at nearby East End before joining the rough gravel roads leading to London.

Ox Drove

71

Thumpers

In the early morning mist of Watership Down the thunder of race-horse hooves echo historic equestrian traditions. King John and the early Norman kings erected a series of hunting lodges in this area for their own sporting enjoyment. Today, Queen Elizabeth II continues this tradition by stabling her race-horses at nearby Park House Stables. Watership Down is also known to millions of children as the homeland of a community of rabbits in Richard Adams' book, 'Watership Down'.

and Gallopers

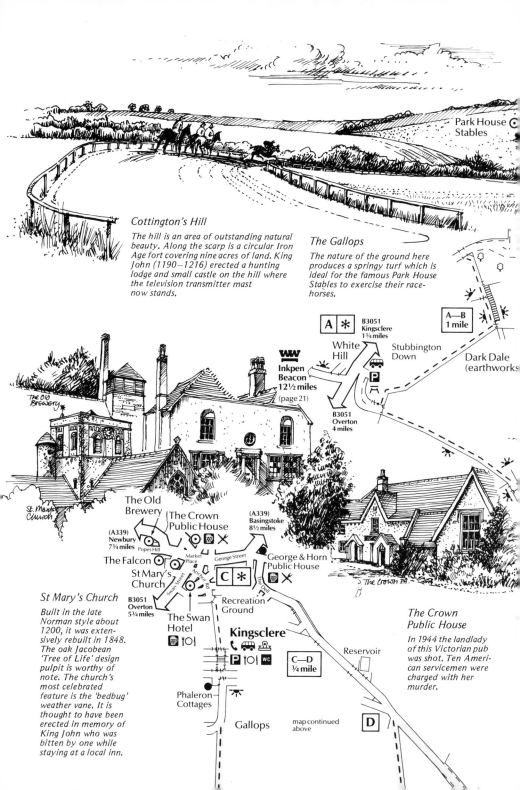

Cottington's Hill

The hill is an area of outstanding natural beauty. Along the scarp is a circular Iron Age fort covering nine acres of land. King John (1190–1216) erected a hunting lodge and small castle on the hill where the television transmitter mast now stands.

The Gallops

The nature of the ground here produces a springy turf which is ideal for the famous Park House Stables to exercise their race-horses.

Park House Stables

A ✳ B3051 Kingsclere 1¾ miles

White Hill

Stubbington Down

A—B 1 mile

Dark Dale (earthworks

Inkpen Beacon 12½ miles (page 21)

B3051 Overton 4 miles

The Old Brewery

St Mary's Church

The Old Brewery

The Crown Public House

(A339) Newbury 7¾ miles

Popes Hill

The Falcon

St Mary's Church

Market Place

George Street

Anchor Rd.

Swan Street

(A339) Basingstoke 8½ miles

George & Horn Public House

The Crown P.H.

C ✳

Recreation Ground

B3051 Overton 5¾ miles

The Swan Hotel

Kingsclere

C—D ¾ mile

Reservoir

D

Phaleron Cottages

Gallops

map continued above

St Mary's Church

Built in the late Norman style about 1200, it was extensively rebuilt in 1848. The oak Jacobean 'Tree of Life' design pulpit is worthy of note. The church's most celebrated feature is the 'bedbug' weather vane. It is thought to have been erected in memory of King John who was bitten by one while staying at a local inn.

The Crown Public House

In 1944 the landlady of this Victorian pub was shot. Ten American servicemen were charged with her murder.

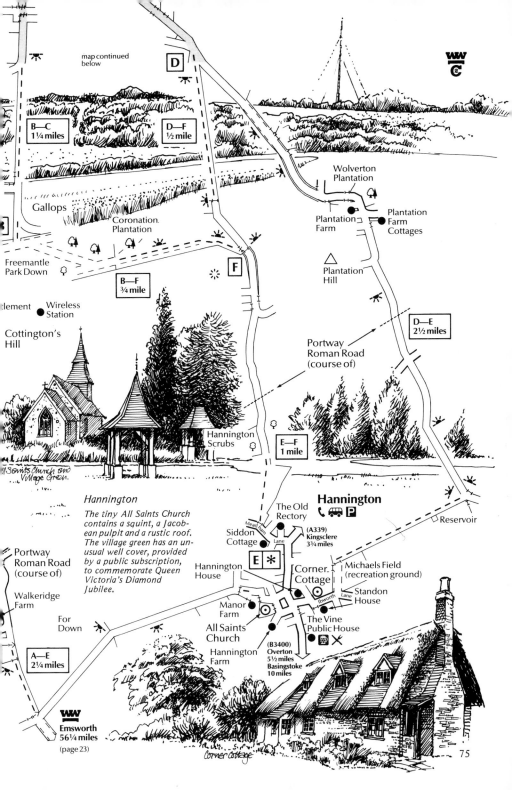

map continued
below

D

W
W
C

B—C
1¼ miles

D—F
½ mile

Gallops

Coronation
Plantation

Wolverton
Plantation

Plantation
Farm

Plantation
Farm
Cottages

Freemantle
Park Down

B—F
¾ mile

F

Plantation
Hill

lement

Wireless
Station

Cottington's
Hill

D—E
2½ miles

Portway
Roman Road
(course of)

Hannington
Scrubs

E—F
1 mile

All Saints Church and
Village Green.

Hannington

*The tiny All Saints Church
contains a squint, a Jacobean pulpit and a rustic roof.
The village green has an unusual well cover, provided
by a public subscription,
to commemorate Queen
Victoria's Diamond
Jubilee.*

The Old
Rectory

Hannington
☎ 🚌 P

Siddon
Cottage

Mead Ham

Lane

(A339)
Kingsclere
3¾ miles

Reservoir

Portway
Roman Road
(course of)

Hannington
House

E *

Corner
Cottage

Ibworth Lane

Michaels Field
(recreation ground)

Standon
House

Walkeridge
Farm

For
Down

Manor
Farm

All Saints
Church

Hannington
Farm

The Vine
Public House
📮 ✗

(B3400)
Overton
5½ miles
Basingstoke
10 miles

A—E
2¼ miles

W
W

Emsworth
56¼ miles

(page 23)

Corner Cottage

75

Abandoned

This is an area of lost or disbanded communities. The prehistoric hill-fort known as Oliver's Battery on Abbotstone Down was built to protect an Iron Age community; only the earthworks remain. Later, the thriving medieval village of Abbotstone was abandoned due, it is thought, to the declining fortunes of the wool trade. On a grander scale is The Grange, a neo-classical mansion occupied by a succession of wealthy landowners and the aristocracy. By the 20th century it had become a ruin, but recent restoration work has preserved the exterior.

abodes at Abbotstone

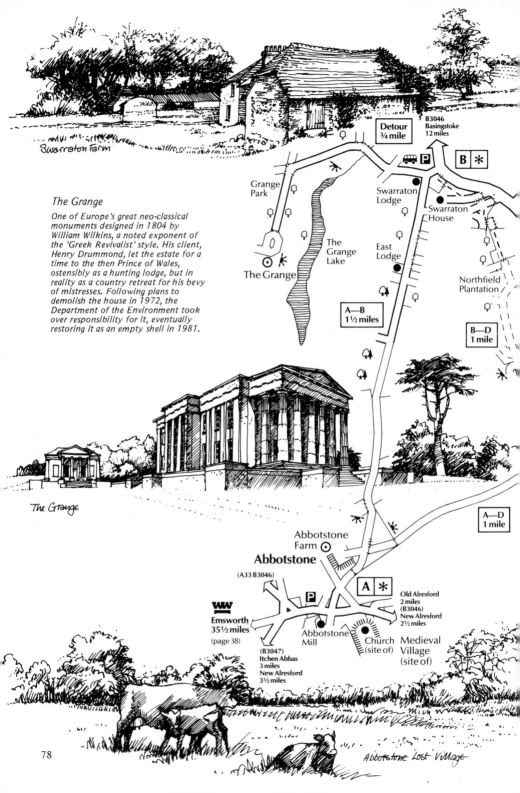

Swarraton Farm

The Grange

One of Europe's great neo-classical monuments designed in 1804 by William Wilkins, a noted exponent of the 'Greek Revivalist' style. His client, Henry Drummond, let the estate for a time to the then Prince of Wales, ostensibly as a hunting lodge, but in reality as a country retreat for his bevy of mistresses. Following plans to demolish the house in 1972, the Department of the Environment took over responsibility for it, eventually restoring it as an empty shell in 1981.

The Grange

Detour ¾ mile

B3046 Basingstoke 12 miles

B ✳

Grange Park

Swarraton Lodge

Swarraton House

The Grange

The Grange Lake

East Lodge

Northfield Plantation

A—B 1½ miles

B—D 1 mile

A—D 1 mile

Abbotstone Farm ☉

Abbotstone

(A33 B3046)

P

A ✳

Old Alresford 2 miles (B3046) New Alresford 2½ miles

Emsworth 35½ miles

(page 38)

(B3047) Itchen Abbas 3 miles New Alresford 3½ miles

Abbotstone Mill

Church (site of)

Medieval Village (site of)

Abbotstone Lost Village

78

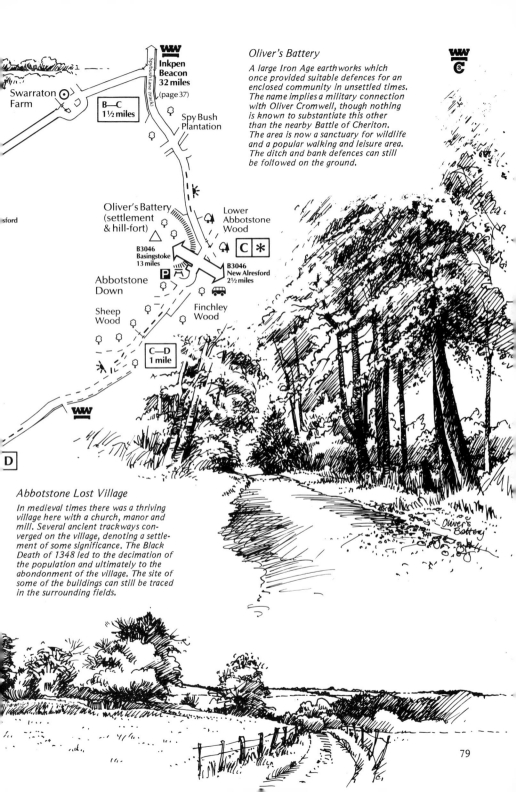

Swarraton Farm

| B—C |
| 1½ miles |

Spybush Lane (track)

Inkpen Beacon 32 miles
(page 37)

Spy Bush Plantation

sford

Oliver's Battery
(settlement & hill-fort)

Lower Abbotstone Wood

B3046 Basingstoke 13 miles

C *

B3046 New Alresford 2½ miles

P

Abbotstone Down

Sheep Wood

Finchley Wood

| C—D |
| 1 mile |

D

Oliver's Battery

A large Iron Age earthworks which once provided suitable defences for an enclosed community in unsettled times. The name implies a military connection with Oliver Cromwell, though nothing is known to substantiate this other than the nearby Battle of Cheriton. The area is now a sanctuary for wildlife and a popular walking and leisure area. The ditch and bank defences can still be followed on the ground.

Oliver's Battery

Abbotstone Lost Village

In medieval times there was a thriving village here with a church, manor and mill. Several ancient trackways converged on the village, denoting a settlement of some significance. The Black Death of 1348 led to the decimation of the population and ultimately to the abondonment of the village. The site of some of the buildings can still be traced in the surrounding fields.

Cheriton's

In 1644, the peaceful fields to the east of Cheriton became the back-drop for the drama of a Civil War engagement. Lord Hopton, supported by the local Tichborne family, represented the Royalist cause, whilst the Parliamentarian battalions were commanded by Sir William Waller. The battle lasted for three hours and resulted in the death of more than two thousand men. Ultimately, this victory altered the course of the War in the Parliamentarian's favour. The Sealed Knot Society dramatically re-enacts this battle annually, on its anniversary.

bloody battle

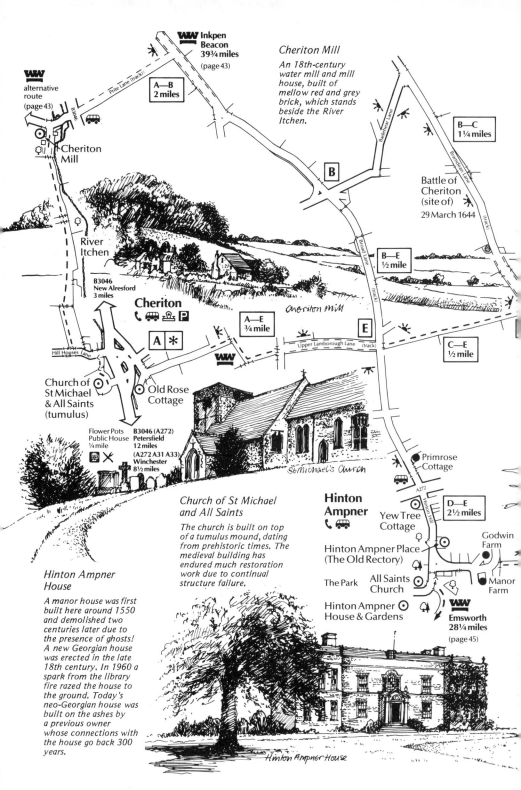

Inkpen Beacon 39¾ miles (page 43)

A—B 2 miles

Prite Lane (track)

B3046

WW alternative route (page 43)

Cheriton Mill

Badgehear Lane

Bramdean Lane

Cheriton Mill

An 18th-century water mill and mill house, built of mellow red and grey brick, which stands beside the River Itchen.

B

B—C 1¼ miles

Battle of Cheriton (site of) 29 March 1644

River Itchen

Broad Lane (track)

B—E ½ mile

B3046 New Alresford 3 miles

Cheriton

cheriton mill

A—E ¾ mile

E

C—E ½ mile

Upper Lamborough Lane (track)

Hill Houses Lane

A *

WW

Church of St Michael & All Saints (tumulus)

Old Rose Cottage

Flower Pots Public House ¼ mile

B3046 (A272) Petersfield 12 miles (A272 A31 A33) Winchester 8½ miles

St Michael's Church

Primrose Cottage

A272

D—E 2½ miles

Hinton Ampner

Yew Tree Cottage

Hinton Hill

Godwin Farm

Hinton Ampner Place (The Old Rectory)

Manor Farm

The Park

All Saints Church

Hinton Ampner House & Gardens

WW **Emsworth** 28¼ miles (page 45)

Church of St Michael and All Saints

The church is built on top of a tumulus mound, dating from prehistoric times. The medieval building has endured much restoration work due to continual structure failure.

Hinton Ampner House

A manor house was first built here around 1550 and demolished two centuries later due to the presence of ghosts! A new Georgian house was erected in the late 18th century. In 1960 a spark from the library fire razed the house to the ground. Today's neo-Georgian house was built on the ashes by a previous owner whose connections with the house go back 300 years.

Hinton Ampner House

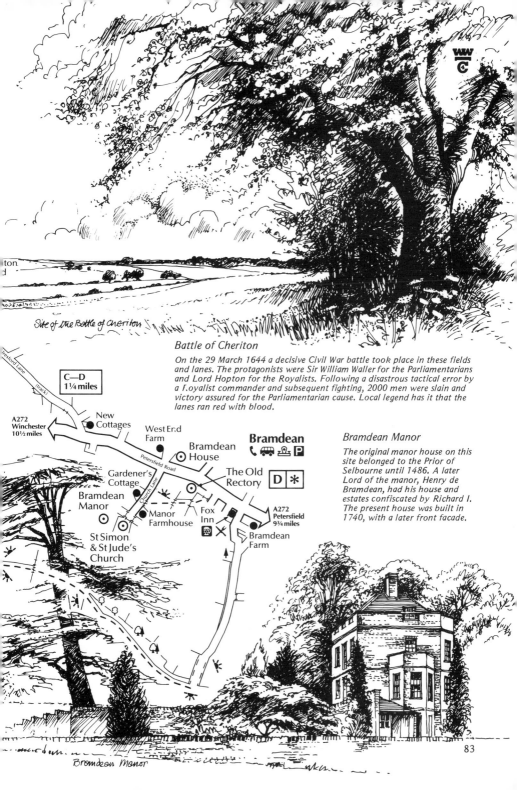

Battle of Cheriton

On the 29 March 1644 a decisive Civil War battle took place in these fields and lanes. The protagonists were Sir William Waller for the Parliamentarians and Lord Hopton for the Royalists. Following a disastrous tactical error by a Royalist commander and subsequent fighting, 2000 men were slain and victory assured for the Parliamentarian cause. Local legend has it that the lanes ran red with blood.

Bramdean Manor

The original manor house on this site belonged to the Prior of Selbourne until 1486. A later Lord of the manor, Henry de Bramdean, had his house and estates confiscated by Richard I. The present house was built in 1740, with a later front facade.

Site of the Battle of Cheriton

Tresford Lane (Track)

C—D
1¼ miles

A272
Winchester
10½ miles

New Cottages

West End Farm

Petersfield Road

Bramdean
House

Bramdean

The Old Rectory

D ✳

Gardener's Cottage

Church Lane

Bramdean Manor

Manor Farmhouse

Fox Inn

A272
Petersfield
9¾ miles

Bramdean Farm

St Simon & St Jude's Church

Bramdean Manor

83

Sanctuary

Old Winchester Hill is a natural vantage point. It was chosen by Iron Age settlers because they preferred the sanctuary afforded by the high ground, to that of the forested swamps of the Meon Valley below. Descent would only be made for hunting purposes, or for military forays. Today the layout of ditches and banks remains unchanged. However, Old Winchester Hill provides for a new kind of sanctuary, one which, under the auspices of the Nature Conservancy Council, protects wildlife and wild flowers.

English Cricket

Ridge Meadow
(Cricket Grou...

Hambledon
Village.

Windmill
△ Down

Hambledon
Vineyard

Hambledon
📞 🚌 🏛 P

Hambledon
National
Schools

St Peter
& St Paul's
Church

Inkpen
Beacon
55¼ miles
(page 55)

A ✳

New Inn

(B2150)
Denmead
3 miles
Droxford
4 miles

West Street

Church Lane

The George
Public House
(George Hotel) ✗

The Coach
House

Stud
Farm

Manor House
(Hambledon
Manor)

Emsworth
14½ miles
(page 55)

Rose
Cottage

A—
1 mile

Hambledon Village and
St Peter and St Paul's Church

*The village, which lies in a valley, is surrounded
by hills whose slopes are clad with groups of
beech trees known locally as 'hangers'. In the
11th century the Saxons built a small church,
some of whose stonework still exists within
the present structure.*

*The village took on the status of a town with
the granting of a market in the 13th century.
This in turn brought wealth to the community
and a gradual enlargement of the church.*

*The 18th-century 'George' is a coaching inn
named after the Prince Regent, who was a
noted cricket enthusiast.*

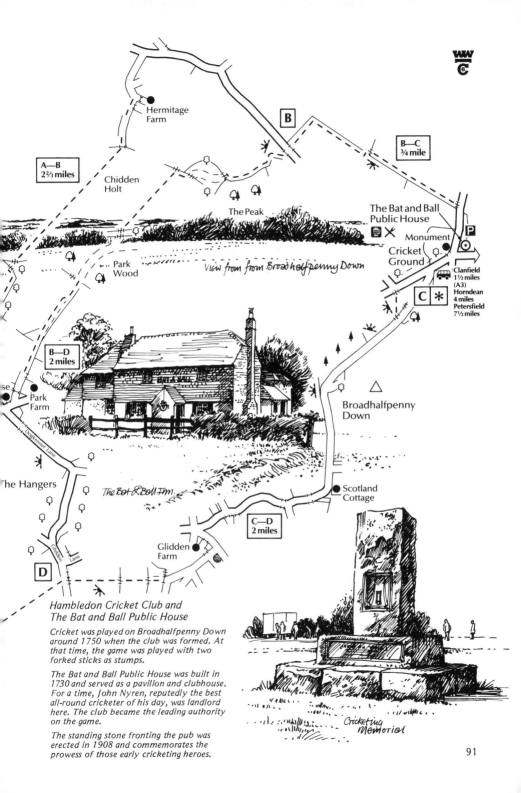

W W
C (compass logo)

Hermitage Farm

B

B—C
¾ mile

A—B
2⅔ miles

Chidden Holt

The Peak

The Bat and Ball Public House

Monument

Cricket Ground

P

Clanfield 1½ miles (A3)
Horndean 4 miles
Petersfield 7½ miles

C *

View from from Broadhalfpenny Down

Park Wood

B—D
2 miles

Broadhalfpenny Down

Park Farm

Dogkennel Lane

The Hangers

The Bat & Ball Inn

Scotland Cottage

Glidden Lane

C—D
2 miles

Glidden Farm

D

Hambledon Cricket Club and The Bat and Ball Public House

Cricket was played on Broadhalfpenny Down around 1750 when the club was formed. At that time, the game was played with two forked sticks as stumps.

The Bat and Ball Public House was built in 1730 and served as a pavilion and clubhouse. For a time, John Nyren, reputedly the best all-round cricketer of his day, was landlord here. The club became the leading authority on the game.

The standing stone fronting the pub was erected in 1908 and commemorates the prowess of those early cricketing heroes.

Cricketing Memorial

91

Information

Ordnance Survey maps
sheet numbers and titles

Landranger Series
scale 1:50000 — 1¼" to the mile

174 Newbury & Wantage
185 Winchester & Basingstoke area
196 Solent & The Isle of Wight
197 Chichester & The Downs

Pathfinder Series
scale 1:25000 — 2½" to the mile

SU 26/36 Hungerford and Savernake
         Forest
SU 45/55 Kingsclere and Ashmansworth
SU 54   Micheldever
SU 43/53 Winchester (North)
         and New Alresford
SU 42/52 Winchester (South)
SU 62/72 Petersfield and East Meon
SU 61/71 Horndean
SU 60/70 Portsmouth and Havant

Transport

Train Services
The following British Rail stations connect with the Wayfarers Walk either within walking distance or by using one of the local bus services. For details of services telephone the appropriate information office.

Newbury and Kintbury
tel: Reading (0734) 595911

Basingstoke, Overton and Micheldever
tel: Basingstoke (0256) 464966

Winchester
tel: Southampton (0703) 229393

Emsworth, Warblington, Havant, Bedhampton and Cosham
tel: Portsmouth (0705) 825771

Bus Services
Information regarding local bus services can be obtained from the Tourist Information Centres

Useful addresses and/ or telephone numbers

Hampshire Recreation
North Hill Close, Andover Road, Winchester, Hampshire SO22 6AQ
tel: Winchester (0962) 846002

Ramblers Association
1/5 Wandsworth Road, London SW8 2XX
tel: 01-582 6878

(RA publishers Ramblers Year Book containing accommodation list)

Weathercall
(up-to-date weather forecast for Hampshire)
tel: 0898 500 403

Youth Hostels

Overton
Youth Hostel, Red Lion Lane, Overton, Basingstoke, Hampshire RG25 3HH
tel: Basingstoke (0256) 770516

OS sheet and grid reference: 185 513495

Winchester
Youth Hostel, The City Mill, 1 Water Lane, Winchester, Hampshire SO23 8EJ
tel: Winchester (0962) 53723

OS sheet and grid reference: 185 486293

Portsmouth
Youth Hostel, Wymering Manor, Cosham, Portsmouth, Hampshire PO6 3NL
tel: Cosham (0705) 375661

OS sheet and grid reference: 196 649055

details of membership from
Youth Hostels Association, Trevelyan House, 8 St Stephen's Hill, St Albans, Hertfordshire AL1 2DY
tel: St Albans (0727) 55215

Tourist information
(including accommodation lists)

Newbury
Tourist Information Centre,
Newbury District Museum, The Wharf,
Newbury, Berkshire RG14 5AS
tel: Newbury (0635) 30267

Basingstoke
Public Relations Officer,
Civic Offices, London Road,
Basingstoke, Hampshire RG21 2AJ
tel: Basingstoke (0256) 56222

Andover
Tourist Information Centre,
Town Mill Car Park, Bridge Street,
Andover, Hampshire
tel: Andover (0264) 24320

Winchester
Tourist Information Centre,
The Guildhall, The Broadway,
Winchester, Hampshire SO23 9JZ
tel: Winchester (0962) 840500

Fareham
Tourist Information Centre,
Ferneham Hall, Osborn Road,
Fareham, Hampshire PO16 7DB
tel: Fareham (0329) 221342

Havant
Tourist Information Centre,
1 Park Road South,
Havant, Hampshire PO9 1HA
tel: Havant (0705) 480024

Places of interest
on or near the Wayfarers Walk

Inkpen Beacon and Walbury Hill
downland and scrub
car park

Highclere Castle, Highclere
tel: Highclere (0635) 253210

Sandham Memorial Chapel
Burghclere, Newbury
tel: Burghclere (063 527) 394

Beacon Hill – hill-fort
downland and scrub
car park and picnic area

White Hill (Watership Down)
downland and scrub
car park and picnic area

The Grange, Northington
(exterior viewing only)

Abbotstone Down – hill-fort
downland and scrub
car park and picnic area

Avington House, Itchen Abbas
tel: Itchen Abbas (096 278) 202

Alresford House, Alresford
tel: Alresford (096 273) 2843

Mid Hants Railway ('Watercress Line')
Alresford Station, Alresford
tel: Alresford (096 273) 3810

Hinton Ampner Gardens
tel: Bramdean (096 279) 344

Old Winchester Hill – hill fort
downland and scrub
car park and picnic area

Hambledon Vineyard
Windmill Down, Hambledon
tel: Hambledon (070 132) 475

Denmead Pottery and Glassworks
Forest Row, Denmead
tel: Waterlooville (0705) 261942

Index

Selected place-names and features only.
Page numbers in **bold** type refer to illustrations.

Acknowledgements

The Wayfarers Walk was conceived, initially, by Hampshire County Recreation Department. This guide has been designed and produced by us, based on an original text by Linda Herbst. We wish to thank a number of friends for their assistance with research during the summer of 1987, especially Sally-Anne Salm (Kingsclere), Greta Bendall (Denmead) and John Stott (Exton). Finally we wish to express our appreciation of the support and encouragement received from Colin Bonsey and his staff at the Hampshire Recreation Department.

Roger Lambert and John Cann

Country code

Enjoy the countryside and respect its life and work

Guard against all risk of fire

Fasten all gates

Keep your dogs under close control

Keep to public paths across farmland

Use gates and stiles to cross fences, hedges and walls

Leave livestock, crops and machinery alone

Take your litter home

Help to keep all water clean

Protect wildlife, plants and trees

Take special care on country roads

Make no unnecessary noise